Pr

St Ignatius
& Pope Francis

by Dermot Mansfield SJ

*All booklets are published thanks to the
generous support of the members of the
Catholic Truth Society*

CATHOLIC TRUTH SOCIETY
PUBLISHERS TO THE HOLY SEE

Contents

All rights reserved. First published as Praying with St Ignatius of Loyola *in 2006 by The Incorporated Catholic Truth Society 40-46 Harleyford Road London SE11 5AY Tel: 020 7640 0042 Fax: 020 7640 0046. This new edition* Praying with St Ignatius & Pope Francis © *2014 The Incorporated Catholic Truth Society.*

ISBN 978 1 86082 915 4

Introduction

Responding to the Love of God

*P*ope Francis, in his interview for Jesuit publications released some six months after his election, has spoken of his favourite image of the Church, as "that of the holy, faithful people of God". A rich and vibrant image for him, it had been put forth prophetically by the Second Vatican Council, which described how we are called as a messianic people by God, and "established by Christ as a communion of life, love and truth". The Council also described how, in consequence of God's choosing, we are "the light of the world and the salt of the earth, sent forth into the whole world".

Such is the vision of Vatican II, as given in its Dogmatic Constitution on the Church, paragraph 9. And for Pope Francis, who so evidently values and relishes personal engagement, "the web of human relationships", as he puts it, is the place where God enters into history - so that "the Church is the people of God on the journey through history, with joys and sorrows".

Chosen as a People and as Individuals

However, if we are chosen as a people, it is because also, in the first place, we are each of us called by name, in an utterly personal and unique way. This personal calling is there for us always, as we exist within the varying networks of relationships that are ours from childhood onwards, and as we travel along the course of our lives. Indeed Jorge Mario Bergolio - to give Pope Francis his own proper name - has had a personal sense, over the years, of being chosen. He has as his motto the Latin words of St Bede the Venerable referring to the call of Matthew, 'Miserando atque Eligendo', which, in accordance with Bede's commentary, can be translated as: "And Jesus, looking on him with the eyes of mercy, chose him". It follows that something like this awareness can be there for each of us. Within the context of all the people that have formed my life, there can arise an acute sense of how God is really there before me, calling me by name - although unworthy and a sinner - and desiring to enter deeply into the house of my heart.

A Jesuit Pope

Of significance is the fact that Pope Francis has been a member of the Jesuit religious order, in its South American province of Argentina. So, while he always remembers the many other influences - and especially the close and warm familial ones - enriching the gift of faith in him, he also remains conscious of how he has been affected by the spirituality of St Ignatius of Loyola, founder of the Jesuits. For, although Ignatius is best known for his role in founding that order in the sixteenth century, nevertheless his greatest significance lies in how he himself deeply experienced God - and then worked out a way, a spirituality, whereby any of us can likewise experience God ourselves, and begin to discern how we are being called and led onward by God.

All this St Ignatius did, interestingly, as a layperson. He was simply an 'ordinary Christian' among God's people, firstly when he had the experience of God invading his life, and secondly when over time he compiled the text which he named the 'Spiritual Exercises'. In the hands of any good guide or director, the set of notes and guidelines comprising the Exercises were intended as the means by which - if we can set aside the required time - we can experience God's presence and calling, and be enabled to live out henceforth the consequences of that blessing. And for Pope Francis then, as a Jesuit and follower of St Ignatius, the spirituality contained in the Spiritual Exercises has been a major influence - he has relied on it for long years, considering it valuable both for himself and for many others in life today. This he has stressed in the interview noted above.

As it happens, this particular introduction to Ignatian spirituality, which you have in your hands, was already published some years ago, under the title, *Praying with St Ignatius of Loyola*. At that time, in 2006, some Jesuit anniversaries were being remembered. There was the 450th anniversary of the death of St Ignatius, who had eventually studied for ordination and lived to see the considerable expansion of the order he named the Society ('Companionship') of Jesus. And secondly, there was the 500th anniversary of the birth of the two earliest companions of Ignatius, namely Francis Xavier and Peter Favre. Of these companions, Francis Xavier is of course the better known, because of the missionary trail he blazed to the East; to India, and Indonesia, and to Japan. But Peter Favre (or Faber) deserves recognition too - and incidentally is deeply revered by Pope Francis. The first priest of the Jesuit order (see the excellent account of him in the CTS *Great Saints* series), Peter tried to bring respect and compassion into the controversies of the Reformation in Germany, and he was also the one Ignatius considered best at giving his own 'Spiritual Exercises' retreat experience.

A Simple Introduction to Ignatian Spirituality

But here we offer these pages again - and principally because of the interest aroused by our present Pope in their subject. The format they contain is simple. At the beginning there is an historical outline of the personal experience of Ignatius, during and after the time of his conversion. After that, a sketch is given of the main features of what is usually termed Ignatian spirituality. Then there is an invitation, as it were, into some actual prayer we might make for ourselves, in accord with the outline of the Spiritual Exercises themselves. And then there is a conclusion, turning once more to the inspiration of Pope Francis.

As was said in the earlier edition, the hope is that you, the reader, may hit upon something encouraging and new in these brief pages. Perhaps, then, the insights or thoughts occurring to you may prove a help in the living out of *your* way, as *you* endeavour to respond, in your particular circumstances, to the love and calling of God. Pope Francis, as is clear from so many of his words and gestures already, would want nothing better of himself or of us. He wants us all to realise how deeply we are part of God's "holy, faithful people" - above all through our ordinary daily human living, where in acts of kindness, with care for truth, and by nurturing the gift of faith, we are drawn into the great mystery of Christ's redeeming love, reaching out to the ends of the earth.

The Way of Ignatius

The Initial Experience of Ignatius Loyola

Ignatius, or Inigo de Loyola, to give him his original family name, lived in very different times to our own. Yet there are basic human and religious aspects to him which ought to relate to any historical period, and which may certainly be considered to speak to our own contemporary and varied experiences of life.

He was born about 1491 into a minor noble family at Loyola, in the hilly Basque country of northern Spain. You will find his story well outlined in the companion booklet to this, *Ignatius of Loyola*, in the CTS *Great Saints* series. Suffice to say here that his promising career as a soldier and at court ended with serious leg injuries sustained in a battle at Pamplona in 1521. But, as has often happened in life, the closing of one door led to the opening of another and much unexpected one. Convalescing in the family castle at Loyola, all he could get for reading to distract him were two books, one *The Life of Christ*, and another on *The Lives of the Saints*. Through mulling over what he read, his tortured and anguished mind found itself opening to new possibilities. What if Christ were actually calling him personally, and to a new way of life, much better than the old? What if he was being invited now to follow the example of the saints he was reading about, such as Francis and Dominic?

Such was the force of his thoughts and emotions that when he arose from his sickbed he felt like a new person, and with a new vision and ideal. Somehow he knew, in very truth, Christ *was* calling him. The awareness of this moreover gave him a peace and a consolation he had never experienced before. He also felt the Virgin Mary's presence, and her encouragement.

What Ignatius was undergoing would be called today a "conversion experience". Any of us might have had elements of that happening to us. Perhaps you were going along nicely in life, taking things for granted. Then the unexpected happened: a crisis maybe. But in time through friends, or reading, or some retreat experience, a new vista opens up, where the world of faith becomes very real, and you can do no other than set out upon the new path opening before your eyes. At any rate, Ignatius certainly underwent some process such as this. He for instance found the gospel stories full of meaning for him, and began to copy out passages from them into a notebook he had acquired. And, recovered somewhat from his injuries, he left behind him the old way of life symbolised by that castle at Loyola, and in early 1522 set out on an uncharted journey as a poor person, a "pilgrim", wanting only to live by the Gospel.

A Second Decisive Experience

However, despite the clarity a new and cherished ideal may bring, it is fairly inevitable that its accomplishment will not be as straightforward as we might like it to be. Ignatius was to discover this rather quickly. On his journey away from home he came to the great Benedictine monastery high up on Montserrat, not far from Barcelona, and kept vigil there, at the famous Catalan shrine of Our Lady. Then he withdrew down the mountain to the town of Manresa, intending to pause and write more gospel passages into his book. But here the consolation he had known deserted him. His consciousness became darkly troublesome instead, and this despite increased prayer and penances. Ten dreadful anguished months followed, and only when he finally heeded the advice of a good Dominican confessor - to ease his fasting and hours of prayer - did the darkness lift. In effect, Ignatius had left behind now a stubborn streak in him, listened to wise guidance, and become more malleable, humble, and transparent. A new joy came to him, together with a great illuminated understanding of the Christian faith, especially the mystery of the Trinity. You could say that he had been led from dependence on his own efforts to a simple and trusting faith in God's initiative and leading. This is certainly not a million miles away from what may happen in our own experience. We can find ourselves led from what is really a focus on self and one's own activity to a humbler reliance on God. This deep change in us is often by way of crisis, and can involve much helplessness and darkness. Someone else's wise suggestions may play a decisive role. And we are led into a gentler and truer way of living our humanity and our faith.

The Composition of the Spiritual Exercises

It is interesting to note what Ignatius did next. He was a practical type of person, and always tried to think out ways of helping anyone who crossed his path. So, drawing on his experiences, he began to compile notes in his copybook on the Christian life and discipleship, which would eventually form the retreat framework of what he called the "Spiritual Exercises". He had found God in his life, turning him around, leading him along the way of Christian discipleship. That same experience, he became convinced, God would offer to others through those Spiritual Exercises. Other people would learn, like him, to look to Christ, to his way, his calling. They would realise the nature of the elemental struggle between good and evil which everyone encounters in life, and through acquiring the gift of discernment as well as being open to God's grace, they would be enabled to make good choices in accord with the mind and heart of Christ. Ultimately, men and women touched by this experience would find themselves growing in love, with the love by which God so loved them in Christ.

The Pilgrim's Onward Journey

Not that all this became clear all at once. For "the pilgrim," as Ignatius called himself, had many years of search and travelling ahead of him, before other aspects of God's calling to him would become clear. In Barcelona, the Holy Land, the universities of Alcala and Salamanca, and then that of Paris, through a variety of events including imprisonment by the Inquisition, Ignatius only slowly found his ultimate vocation. In 1534 in Paris, he and a little group of companions which had gathered around him, including Peter Favre and Francis Xavier, vowed to live together a simple evangelical and Christian way of life. At first they thought this might entail living in the Holy Land itself. But in time they realised they were being drawn more directly into the service of the Catholic Church, and should put themselves in Rome at the disposal of the Pope. Ordained as priests, by 1540 they had formed the nucleus of a new religious order, the Society of Jesus. The dimension of the Church, and service within it, became very important to them, therefore, and yet in such a way that they should find themselves in freedom disposed for a multitude of works and ministries, such as the times required.

So it was that Ignatius, "the pilgrim", who as a layman formerly had led many people to the experience of God, opened up for them both by the manner of his life and his conversations, as well as by making his Spiritual Exercises, now found himself in Rome with a quite different role: as a priest at the head of the growing Society of Jesus, involved in administrative work, long letter writing, and having endless dealings with his companions, churchmen, princes, and the papacy. He also wrote the Constitutions for the order. And in 1556, on 31st July, he died quietly and alone, leaving behind him an already well-established legacy.

———◆———

Spiritual Legacy of Ignatius

Central Traits of Ignatian Spirituality

At this point we can pause, in order to look at some of the main aspects of the spiritual legacy of Ignatius. What would he tell us today, out of what he experienced? How would he show us that his story and insights are relevant for the challenges we are facing in our twenty-first century?

Above all, Ignatius would tell us, that just as he had direct experience of God, so can we too. The same living God, author of our lives, is always before us. This was the overwhelming reality for Ignatius, and it can be for us too. Also, as we have seen, Ignatius for long years on his spiritual journey was a layperson. He could say to us therefore that none of us requires any exalted status, clerical or otherwise, for God to touch our lives. God comes to us directly, to where we are, and to us just as we are. And it was as a layperson that Ignatius the pilgrim would journey for those many years, and would, like any man or woman who tries to live the Christian life, enter the further reaches of God's loving purposes only through the many trials and errors, successes and failures, and troubles and joys encountered, as life unfolds.

Without a doubt, he would want us to acquire the art of "discerning the spirits". This was a huge learning for Ignatius. As we saw, in the middle of his conversion experience he had noticed within himself a special gift of consolation and peace. This was in a context where, on his sick bed, he found himself pulled in different directions. Which way was God's way? By noticing the difference of the "spirits" or influences pulling at his heart, he began to glimpse how God was moving him.

What Ignatius learned was that God's spirit moving within him was a consoling and encouraging presence - whereas the spirit opposite to God was a desolating one, which when it affected him left him empty and downcast. Thus, as he considered the gospels and the vision they offered him, he was steadily consoled. But when he doubted their reality, and instead tried to rake up the idea of his old career ambitions, he found himself in desolation. He learned so much from that simple but vital distinction - and so can we. Noticing the effects of consolation and desolation playing upon our hearts, and abiding by the enlightenment given in authentic consolation, is a great help to our making the best possible choices about our lives, in accord with the promptings of God.

Naturally, all this presupposes a great *desire* on our part: our desire above everything else in life for the goodness and truth of God. Ignatius placed great store on this deepest desire of our hearts. He knew that this desire would arise in "a humbled contrite heart" (*Ps* 51), and one filled with gratitude for endless forgiving grace. But also - and this is crucial for authentic discernment - Ignatius knew that the grace of God was none other than this: our being brought into the real and loving presence of Christ. Jesus is the Living One, always with us, before us. His presence is consolation. If we truly desire him, or at least wish to desire him with all our hearts, then we find that he is already looking at us, regarding us in love. Furthermore, although in his sight we can be acutely conscious of our weakness, we each of us hear him calling us by our name, calling us into relationship with him, into a life of discipleship and joy. Our looking to Jesus, therefore, and our wish to abide in him, and follow his call, becomes the touchstone for genuine discernment and choice. Ignatius would urge this looking, this "contemplation", upon us today. And he would remind us that the values of Jesus, as we find them in the gospels, are the surest and safest guidelines we can ever know.

To the Heart of the Matter

Really, when you think of it, what we are considering here is at the centre of the gospels and the whole New Testament. Indeed any true spirituality, modern or ancient, leads us in this direction. Put simply, then, if you follow the invitation of Ignatius, especially by making his Spiritual Exercises in some form or other, you are drawn by your very own desire to grow in greater and greater love and knowledge of Jesus. You do that by learning to look at him in the gospel stories, in the infancy ones first of all, and then in the events of Jesus's active ministry.

This is by way of an imaginative prayer of contemplation. Such prayer is set against the background of the Incarnation. We are asked, first of all, to picture for ourselves a great canvas: how the Blessed Trinity looks upon our needy world, determining to send for its healing the Second Person, who will be born as one of us through Mary's "yes" in Nazareth. Following from this perspective of Trinitarian love, we are drawn into the mystery of the various gospel scenes, their living reality, their simple humanity, and are captivated by what we see. Just as Ignatius, along with those who made the Exercises under him, was in his praying utterly moved by what he saw and experienced in those events, so can we be too. We can learn in a deeply moving way what it is to be a Christian therefore, in a manner akin to that of the original disciples of Jesus.

Indeed, the whole issue is one of discipleship, of following concretely in our lives here and now the way of the gospels. This is where, for the practical and realistic Ignatius, actual decisions must follow from our contemplating. Enveloped in the loving and truthful atmosphere of the gospels, we are also led in the Exercises to consider the consequences and choices about our actual living. This could include, if we are free and drawn to do so, embracing in some form the simple and evangelical manner of life represented by Jesus's own.

Here there is set before us a "Mediation on Two Standards," outlining in a picturesque battlefield scenario what can be played out in human hearts. For as we look at the real possibilities facing us in life, Ignatius expects that the elemental struggle between what is of God and what is opposite to him will become highlighted within us. We can be buffeted to and fro. So here we are asked to discern well, in order to choose well. And the criterion of it all, to say it again, is the heartfelt knowledge and love of Christ, who himself in his life was poor and humble. We are drawn to him, attracted to him and his manner of life. And so whatever form our own discipleship with him takes, we will certainly find ourselves drawn in spirit "to walk in the way in which he walked" (1 *Jn* 2:6). Our way can be none other than that of the Beatitudes, of the poor in spirit.

Love is God's Meaning

As in the gospels, so in the Exercises there is a movement towards what we call the Paschal Mystery. Christian discipleship after all, our walking with Christ, leads us to that place where, "having loved his own in the world, he loved them to the end" (*Jn* 13:1). We are asked therefore by Ignatius to contemplate Christ suffering, rejected, and brought to death. Our love bids us do this. And, mysteriously, our own following along the road of discipleship will surely bring some aspect of the Paschal Mystery into our lives. It cannot be otherwise, for that is the way of redemptive love. Around this time of prayer as well, we become very conscious of Mary, who witnessed what was done to her son.

Our faith however is an Easter faith. The fullness of our experience of the Paschal Mystery is our belief in Jesus who, beyond darkness and death and the grave, is risen and abidingly present to us. So Ignatius leads us into the utterly graced experience of being with Jesus in the gladness and joy of his Resurrection. Again Mary is present with us. We contemplate the gospel resurrection scenes, open to their grace of gladness, born out of darkness and abandonment. And what the disciples came to realise then we know will be true for us: always along our Christian journey we have the risen, living Lord with us, who goes before us even as he sends us out, and whose gift is joy.

Finally, and to sum up the graces of the Spiritual Exercises, we are led simply into a prayer of love, in what is termed the "Contemplation to Attain the Love of God". Here, we find ourselves invited to go forward into the rest of our life by means of the gift of divine love, which is and will be poured endlessly into our hearts all our life long. The horizon we look out upon henceforth can never be other than this, wherever we are, whatever we do. For "love is God's meaning in everything," as Julian of Norwich heard, and wrote in her *Revelations of Divine Love*, long before Ignatius. And for Ignatius at the end of the Exercises that love, and the response of our own hearts to its overwhelming giftedness, determines how we will walk henceforth, along the pathways before us, all our days.

Praying with Ignatius

Hopefully the above paragraphs, although they are rather compressed, give some taste of what is contained in Ignatian spirituality. I have tried to show that, at its best, it goes to "the heart of the matter", to the heart of the New Testament. I do not wish however to imply that it does so in some exclusive or privileged sense. There are other forms of spirituality equally or perhaps more valid. You could think of the great Benedictine inspiration for living the Christian life, for instance. Again, the Franciscan and Carmelite spiritualities, to name some other principal ones from the past, today are offering rich inspiration for prayer and living. In any case all of these are really only means, or avenues of approach, pointing us toward the mystery of Christ and Christian discipleship. It could be that you need none of these means. After all, the Eucharist and the Church's liturgical year draw us most powerfully into the depths of the same mystery - and all the various authentic spiritualities must point us in the direction of that ecclesial and eucharistic way of living the gospels. Such spiritualities simply provide various useful personal and tangible frameworks for living out our faith.

It is worth remarking that one valuable feature of the Spiritual Exercises is flexibility. The very nature of the book, which is really a set of notes put together by Ignatius, as we have seen already, is one of adjustment to personal needs and circumstances. It is in fact intended for the use of an experienced director or guide, who will help an individual personally to find the way God is leading him or her, and especially nowadays through a thoughtful choice of suitable scripture for prayer.

Note this: the Exercises require wise and experienced personal guidance, as they were composed to be inherently adaptable to different needs and circumstances. Therefore they invite to great *freedom*: the freedom of the director to respect and truly listen to the person seeking God, and the freedom of that person (the retreatant or "exercitant") to be who they really are, while desiring to be interiorly open in their heart to the loving promptings and call of God. Ignatius really did envisage this way, and no other, for the giving and making of his Spiritual Exercises. Unfortunately, often in the past that aspect of personal freedom was lost sight of. But thankfully in recent times it has been in large measure recovered.

Thirty Day Retreat

Concretely, then, in what shape or form might you make the Spiritual Exercises today? Well, their classical format unfolds in what is known as the "Thirty-Day Retreat". This is where people set aside a full month and give themselves totally to the experience, in some such place as St Beuno's in North Wales, or Loyola Hall at Rainhill near Liverpool, or Manresa House at Dollymount in Dublin. Key elements include a special atmosphere of quiet, the supportive presence of other like-minded praying people, and valuable personal direction provided each day. But obviously this intensive kind of retreat, although ideal in many ways, can only be a realistic option for very few individuals.

Exercises in Daily Life

More suitable to many modern circumstances is what is known as the "Exercises in Daily Life". Ignatius saw this as a real possibility, even in his time. In essence, as the title suggests, you make the Exercises in the midst of your daily living. You set aside a time for prayer each day, working out the details of that with your chosen director, who will meet with you about once a week to provide personal guidance. So instead of thirty days of intensive prayer, there will be something like thirty weeks devoted to the Exercises - nearly eight months therefore, perhaps conveniently stretching from September or October around to the month of May. A great advantage of the Exercises in Daily Life is precisely that the experience is rooted in the down-to-earth realities of everyday living. The scripture material used, and the Ignatian themes, will then be tested and tried amidst life's actual challenges, and in consequence can be all the more effective.

Individually Guided Retreat

But the Exercises have inspired many other kinds of retreat experience. The "Individually Guided Retreat", scripture-based, and lasting usually for six or eight days, has grown out of the Exercises. It has been very much sought after for many years now, and was pioneered in Jesuit centres like St Beuno's and the others noted above. But many more retreat houses in the U.K. and in Ireland provide opportunities for such an experience. Mention should also be made of Weekend Retreats, which of course take many forms. Historically, such retreats started as yet another adaptation of the Exercises, providing opportunities for a wider range of people, and who could manage no more than one or two nights away from home.

A Special Way: the Parish Weeks of Guided Prayer

However, the last number of years have seen the spread of one of the most valuable adaptations of the Exercises, namely the Parish-based form of Individually Guided Retreat, taking place usually over a week, or else over four or six weeks. Spreading from Canada to Ireland in 1985, and then to Britain, these retreats now take place on the different continents, in countries in Africa, South America, and Asia, for instance. Especially for people living in poor and marginalised circumstances, these simple yet deep retreats have provided a long-sought after and encouraging introduction to scriptural prayer, and to the privilege of being listened to and directed by wise and competent spiritual guides. But they have not been confined to any one social milieu. And, importantly, they often have an ecumenical dimension as well (indeed, a rather similar form of retreat has been developed independently in the Anglican diocese of Southwark, in South London).

For the strength of these retreats is that they take place in the very places where people struggle and live. It is out of the question for most men and women to get to a retreat centre. Instead, with this form of experience the "retreat comes to you", so to speak. Take as an example where an actual week's experience is arranged. You find yourself at a parish venue, perhaps your local school. After an introductory meeting on a Sunday night, you spend a while each day praying with a selected gospel passage, and then you have a personal chat each evening with your own guide. You run into some of the others coming and going to their guides (and hopefully you have time to stop with some of them for a cuppa in the tearoom!). Through it all, something important happens over the week. You find the gospels perhaps coming to life in a way they didn't before, casting a special light on your life. You value the personal meeting with your guide, especially how you are listened to, and respected. And at a concluding meeting of all concerned, on the Saturday evening, hopefully you find yourself confirmed and strengthened through hearing a little of the experiences of others, and you go out with some helpful guidelines for the future.

As I have said, this basic and yet inspired type of "home-based" retreat has proved to be most valuable today. Many people in very different settings have testified to the help and encouragement they have received through them. Schools have used them at well, with thoughtful pupils enriched by their experience. And again it is worth mentioning their ecumenical worth, as people from different Churches can come together in a common love of the scriptures and of prayer. In any case, despite unpromising beginnings during the great religious conflict of the Reformation, generally Ignatian spirituality has moved well and easily into the ecumenical field in modern times.

Suggestions for Prayer

At this juncture we can do nothing better than pass beyond ideas and enter into prayer itself. Long ago the Catholic author Hillaire Belloc ended a little book on sailing with the words: "And now, dear reader, read less and sail more!" So with his advice in mind, and translating it to the realm of spirituality let me select a few points from the Spiritual Exercises that will help us pause for a moment, ponder, and pray.

1. The Principal and Foundation

At the very beginning of the Exercises there is a text called "The Principal and Foundation". In it, we are invited to bring into focus the deepest reality about our human life: each of us is made for God, and everything else in life is meant to have that end in view. As a way of fleshing out its meaning, I suggest having a look at the beautiful lines of Psalm 61, which begins: "O God, you are my God, for you I long, for you my soul is thirsting". *Lord my God, help me to understand how my restless heart is made for you, and will only find its fulfilment in you. Help me to desire you, to desire all your truth and goodness and beauty, with all my heart.*

2. The Call of Christ

Further on, in the meditation "The Call Christ", Ignatius desires me to realise how Christ is calling me now. Although weak and sinful, I am looked on in love by him. And he is calling me to be in some way *with* him, to be part of his work of redemptive love here and now in the world. Picture in imagination Jesus, who is the Good Shepherd (*Jn* 10), whose voice we hear, who leads to safe pastures. *Lord of my heart, you are always there before me. Let me hear your voice, in every situation of my life, and let me follow the longing within me to be with you.*

3. Contemplations of Christ

The various "Contemplations of Christ" in the Exercises invite us to look at and ponder the gospel mysteries. Each scene is actually before us: for instance the little child born to Mary, later on the grown Jesus proclaiming the Kingdom on the mountainside, or calling his disciples, walking on the waters of the lake of Galilee, or with the woman at the well in Samaria. Let me look at him, for he is really present to me in these mysteries. *Jesus, as I contemplate you, speaking, healing, moving among people, help my understanding of you to grow deeply, so I may love you more, and follow you more closely.*

4. Two Standards

In the "Two Standards" meditation, as mentioned already, there is a realistic portrayal of the primordial struggle between two sets of loyalties, which is waged in every walk of life and in every heart. One way, although alluring, leads to deathly self-centredness and pride. But the way to true life, by contrast, is centred on the attractiveness of Christ, and brings me by way of the Beatitudes to poverty of spirit and humility. I might recall again the Good Shepherd (Jn 10). *Lord, when I am pulled to and fro, help me in all things to listen to your voice, and to be led by your example and words - for in this way alone will I come to inner freedom and peace. Give me, therefore, a wise and discerning heart.*

5. Paschal Mystery

The movement of the Exercises, as we have seen, brings us to prayer within the Paschal Mystery. We contemplate the institution of the Eucharist, and we are drawn to accompany Christ in his suffering, and in his dying on the Cross. This drawing is the instinct of all loving Christian devotion. Especially today, it leads us too into the suffering and rejection people endure in our world - in them, Christ is crying out from all the ends of the earth. But also, as the disciples were, we are being led from such depths and dereliction to resurrection faith. For Christ is now and always the living One, who dies no more, who comes to us always "as one who consoles". *Jesus, let me always run to the love you offer in your Passion. May I be strengthened in all I do by your suffering and dying. Expand my heart, help me reach out to every stranger, to all who are despised and rejected. And lead me, together with those who are dear to me, into enduring Resurrection hope and joy.*

The Awareness Examen

———⊷◄►⊶———

There is yet one other form of prayer Ignatius gave us, and which some would consider the best heritage this thoughtful "pilgrim" has left us, for our own day-to-day living, as we journey onwards. In his wish for us to become discerning persons, he recommended that every day we pause for prayer, and reflect on the events of the day and their meaning for us. It is variously called the Consciousness Examen, or the Awareness Examen, and has five parts to it. Usually it is best made in the evening. Again, in noting the following outline, some actual reflection and prayer is best.

1. Recollection

Firstly, recollecting myself in God's presence, I think of the day just past, and give thanks. It has been a gift, for God is always gifting me. And thankfulness itself is a great gift. *Lord, thank you for your gifts, for your presence this day. Thank you too for the wonder of my being.*

2. Light

Secondly, I pray for light, in order to reflect more deeply. *O Holy Spirit, giver of wisdom, grant me light, give me a discerning heart.*

3. Examen

Thirdly, I look back over the day, and "examine" it, so to speak. I notice where God has indeed come to me: through a person, in someone's courtesy, or in something I read, or nature's beauty, or in an experience of prayer. In other words, I note the moments of grace, and where my own actions and responses have been good and grace-filled. But also I try to see where my response to events and people has been less than good. Where have I overlooked something, or failed to listen, or have not reached out to someone in need? Perhaps, then, I realise ways in which I have been neglectful, negative.

4. Contrition

Fourthly, then, with a contrite heart I turn towards the Lord's mercy. *Have mercy on me, Lord, in your kindness. Heal me of my sins and weaknesses. In the secret of my heart, teach me humility and wisdom.*

5. The Future

Fifthly, I conclude my prayer by looking forward, towards tomorrow, and to the future. I do so, in consolation, by summoning up great hope in God's love, present to me now, and always there for me along the road ahead. *Lord, thank you for your presence and healing. Truly I know you go before me always. Let me therefore see you present in all things. Allow me to receive your gift of hope, and to bring hope to those I meet along the path ahead. Amen.*

Conclusion

Drawn to the Heart of the Gospel

As these pages draw to a close, it should be emphasised that Ignatius placed great store on daily reflective prayer, such as that we have outlined above. The reflective prayer of awareness is indeed the right prayer for those who journey. For if I see things rightly, I realise I too am a "pilgrim", just as Ignatius was. Therefore, as I travel, it is very right to be open and attentive to the ways of God's leading. What is really happening in my life? Where especially can I hear the voice of the "Good Shepherd" calling to me, calling me by name? Hearing this gracious voice, indeed, in the varied circumstances of my life, and in my heart, can be so encouraging - "The sheep that belong to me listen to my voice. I know them, and they follow me" (*Jn* 10:27). So, by being prayerfully reflective and watchful, day by day, I will become more aware of Christ's living presence in my life. I will hear the words he speaks to me, and discern the way he leads me.

Pope Francis has spoken about this gift of a discerning heart, so valuable to us as we journey. He urges us to be humble and open as we go forward, "seeking and finding God in all things". "Our life" the Pope says, "is not given to us like an opera libretto, in which all is written down; but it means going, walking, doing, searching, seeing…We must enter into the adventure of the quest for meeting God; we must let God search and encounter us".

Yet, as was said at the beginning, although the quest is intimately personal, we do not just by ourselves alone find God. For implied in Ignatian spirituality is a feeling for and 'sense' of Christ's own Church, such that I cannot discern without some openness to and participation in the mystery of the Church and its Eucharist. It is in this context of discernment that Pope Francis, following Vatican II, has spoken of the Church as "the holy, faithful people of God". Therefore, while he echoes Ignatius in urging us "to think with the Church" - which is of its nature "hierarchical" - nevertheless he reminds us that the Church to which we adhere is, first and foremost, "the people of God, pastors and people together". Our discernment as a consequence will align us with the "supernatural sense of the faith of all the people walking together".

One perhaps surprising point can be added here. In taking the name 'Francis', the Pope was taking that of the great saint of the Middle Ages. "Don't forget the poor!" he heard from a Franciscan Cardinal friend at the time of his election. At that moment, he tells us, the name of Francis came to him. And, as he thought too of all the wars in the world, once again the same name came into his heart - Francis of Assisi, lover of the poor, and a man of peace. Now, what is interesting here is that the spirituality of St Francis of Assisi, already three hundred years in existence, actually had a profound effect on the sixteenth-century St Ignatius of Loyola. There were Franciscan influences, for instance, in his family background, and there was what could be called the aura of St Francis of Assisi in the books he read at the time of his conversion.

We cannot here go into all the strands of influence of Francis of Assisi on Ignatius. But what we must say is that these two saints, from quite different eras, were very united in what matters. In complementary ways, both of them invite us to contemplate the figure of Christ offered us in the Gospels. And they especially invite us to contemplate and ponder that "love to the end" manifested in the person of Christ Crucified. Again, they are also one in their urging us to live an authentic discipleship, in whatever manner of life is right for us, according to the spirit of the Beatitudes.

All this remains the challenge and call today. In addition, by living with the spirit of the Beatitudes, in our contemporary world, we can see how any loving following of "Christ poor and humble" will lead to an awareness of, and union with, all the poor on this earth. "Don't forget the poor!" Pope Francis heard - and in turn he keeps addressing those words to us. Therefore, in some way or another, our hearts will move us to be involved in "the struggle for justice and love in the world of today", as Pope Francis's predecessor, Benedict XVI, had put it in his encyclical, *Deus Caritas Est*.

And finally, to sum up what these pages have tried to articulate: we can say that Ignatian spirituality - as part of all good Christian life, where we are among

God's people and are nourished by the Eucharist - simply helps us to abide at the heart of the Gospel. That place and heart becomes our daily living reality. It is there we receive truth and life. There we experience the depths of God. And there, in companionship with all who live in the knowledge and love of Christ, we are increasingly drawn "to act justly, love tenderly, and walk humbly with God" (*Mi* 6:8).

Two prayers

As an appendix, two prayers from the Spiritual Exercises are offered. "Take, Lord, and receive" is from the Contemplation to Attain Love, which ends the experience of the Exercises. "Soul of Christ" is set at the beginning, as a kind of preface. Known as the *Anima Christi*, it is sometimes attributed to Ignatius, but in fact it comes from before his time.

A prayer of love

Take, Lord, and receive
All my liberty, my memory,
My understanding, my entire will
 - All that I have and possess.
You, Lord, have given everything to me.
I now return it to you, O Lord. All is yours.
Dispose of it according to your will.
Give me simply your love and your grace,
And that is enough for me.

The 'Anima Christi'

Soul of Christ, sanctify me.
Body of Christ, save me.
Blood of Christ, inebriate me.
Water from the side of Christ, wash me.
Passion of Christ, strengthen me.
O good Jesus, hear me.
Within your wounds hide me.
Let me never be separated from you.
From the malignant enemy defend me.
At the hour of my death call me,
And bid me come to you,
That with your saints I may praise you
Forever and ever. Amen.